How to Get Your First 1,000 Instagram Followers

A Step-by-Step Guide to Growing a Loyal Audience With Visual Content Strategy, Hashtags, Influencer Collabs, Viral Trends, and More

The Fix-It Guy

Copyright © The Fix-It Guy

All rights reserved. No part of this publication may be reproduced, distributed, or transmitted in any form or by any means, including photocopying, recording, or other electronic or mechanical methods, without the prior written permission of the publisher, except in the case of brief quotations embodied in critical reviews and certain other noncommercial uses permitted by copyright law.

This book is a work of non-fiction, depending on the genre. Any resemblance to actual persons, living or dead, or actual events is purely coincidental.

Table of Contents

Introduction   5
Chapter 1   7
Building a Foundation   7
   Creating a Compelling Instagram Profile   7
   Optimizing Your Bio for Maximum Impact   11
   Choosing the Right Profile Picture   14
Chapter 2   17
Crafting Captivating Visual Content   17
   The Power of Visual Storytelling   17
   Design Tips for Stunning Posts   20
   Utilizing Instagram's Features (Stories, Reels, IGTV) 23
Chapter 3   27
Developing a Content Strategy   27
   Identifying Your Target Audience   27
   Planning a Consistent Posting Schedule   30
   Balancing Content Variety for Engagement   33
Chapter 4   37
Mastering Hashtags   37
   Understanding the Role of Hashtags   37
   Researching and Choosing Effective Hashtags   40
   Creating Your Own Branded Hashtag   43
Chapter 5   47
Leveraging Influencer Collaborations   47
   Finding and Connecting with Relevant Influencers 47
   Negotiating Effective Collaborations   51
   Maximizing the Impact of Influencer Partnerships 54

Chapter 6   **57**
Riding the Wave of Viral Trends   **57**
    Identifying and Participating in Viral Challenges   57
    Capitalizing on Trending Topics   61
    Staying Authentic While Riding Trends   64
Chapter 7   **67**
Engaging with Your Audience   **67**
    Responding to Comments and Direct Messages   67
    Running Contests and Giveaways   70
    Hosting Live Q&A Sessions and Polls   74
Chapter 8   **77**
Analyzing and Adjusting   **77**
    Monitoring Instagram Insights   77
    Analyzing Key Metrics for Growth   81
    Adjusting Your Strategy Based on Data   85
Chapter 9   **89**
Troubleshooting Common Challenges   **89**
    Dealing with Algorithm Changes   89
    Overcoming Plateaus in Growth   94
    Handling Negative Comments and Feedback   98
Conclusion   **103**

Introduction

Hey there, Insta-enthusiasts! Ready to turn your Instagram game from "meh" to "yeah!"? Whether you're a selfie sensation, a foodie fanatic, or just someone who wants their pet iguana to be the next big sensation, you've landed on the right page. Welcome to "How to Get Your First 1,000 Instagram Followers: A Step-by-Step Guide to Growing a Loyal Audience With Visual Content Strategy, Hashtags, Influencer Collabs, Viral Trends, and More."

Imagine this: You post a photo of your avocado toast masterpiece, and suddenly, the world goes wild! Hundreds, no, thousands of followers pouring in, double-tapping their way into your virtual fan club. But wait, you're not a Kardashian, right? No worries. This book is your backstage pass to Instagram stardom, minus the drama.

So, why should you care about gaining followers? Well, aside from the ego boost that comes with having a legion of admirers, there's real power in a thriving Instagram presence. Whether you're a budding influencer, a small business owner, or just an everyday adventurer, your audience on Instagram can transform from a handful to a horde with the right strategies.

We're not here to sell you a one-size-fits-all, magic-beans solution. Nope, this is a practical, step-by-step guide that spills the tea on how to build your tribe the right way. From crafting killer captions to riding the wave of viral trends, we've got your back.

Think of this book as your Instagram fairy godparent, here to guide you through the maze of filters, hashtags, and algorithm mysteries. Are you ready to turn those double taps into a standing ovation? Buckle up, because we're about to embark on a journey that'll make your Instagram dreams hashtag reality!

Chapter 1

Building a Foundation

Creating a Compelling Instagram Profile

Welcome to the starting line, Insta-Champion! Today, we're donning our construction hats and laying the groundwork for your Instagram empire. In this chapter, we'll focus on the first crucial step: Creating a Compelling Instagram Profile. Think of this as the dazzling front door to your online kingdom – you want it to make people stop, stare, and hit that follow button like it owes them money.

Step 1: Profile Pic Magic
Start by choosing a photo that screams "You." This isn't a passport photo, it's a chance to show off your personality. Whether you're smizing like Tyra Banks or giving off "effortless cool," make sure it's a snapshot of the real you.

Troubleshooting: "Help! I can't choose between my cat and that glorious sunset pic!" No worries. If you're torn, go for a pic that shows your face clearly. People connect with faces, not fur.

Step 2: Crafting an Irresistible Bio
Next, you'll want to craft a bio that's short, sweet, and packed with personality.* Think of it as your virtual pick-up line. Who are you, and what's your vibe? Are you a pizza enthusiast? Do you dream of being a plant parent? Spill the beans, and let your quirks shine!

Troubleshooting: "I'm not Shakespeare; I can't bio!" Fear not, my friend. Keep it simple. If you're stuck, ask a friend what they'd say about you in 20 words or less. You might discover you're secretly a superhero with a penchant for witty one-liners.

Step 3: Contact Buttons - Make It Easy Peasy
Now, let's talk contact buttons. Instagram gives you options like email, phone, or your shop. Choose wisely based on your goals. If you're hustling your art, link to your Etsy store. If you're just here for the memes, an email or DM option works wonders.

Troubleshooting: "But what if I get spam emails?" Ah, the internet, where spam flows like water. If it becomes an issue, consider creating a separate email just for your Insta adventures. Problem solved!

8

Step 4: Link in Bio Strategy

The infamous "Link in Bio." You've seen it a million times, and now it's your turn. Whether it's your latest blog post, your YouTube channel, or just that hilarious cat video you found, make it count. Update it regularly to keep things fresh.

Troubleshooting: "I have too many things to link!" Linktr.ee is your new BFF. It lets you create a mini landing page with all your links. Problem solved, and you're officially a link maestro.

Key Takeaways
- Your profile pic is your first impression; make it memorable.
- Your bio is your virtual elevator pitch; keep it fun and true to you.
- Make contacting you a breeze with the right buttons.
- Master the art of the "Link in Bio" for easy navigation.

Now go, dear reader, and let the profile-pimping begin! In the next chapter, we'll dive into the wonderful world of crafting content that'll have people hitting the follow button faster than you can say "Instagram sensation." Get ready to dazzle!

Optimizing Your Bio for Maximum Impact

Alright, Maverick of the Gram, it's time to whip that bio into shape! Your Instagram bio is like the trailer to your life movie, it needs to be short, intriguing, and leave 'em wanting more. Let's dive into the art of Crafting an Irresistible Bio for Maximum Impact.

1. Unleash Your Personality
Your bio is not the place for monotony. Let your personality shine through like sunshine on a beach day. Are you a pun champion? A wanderer with a penchant for dad jokes? Say it loud and proud. Remember, your potential followers are looking for a connection, not a robotic resume.

Troubleshooting: "I'm as interesting as plain toast!" Nonsense! Ask friends what makes you stand out. Embrace the quirks, my friend. You're not just toast; you're avocado toast with extra guac.

2. Drop the Essentials Like It's Hot
Who are you, and what's your deal? Whether you're a dog whisperer, a coffee addict, or a dance-in-the-mirror enthusiast, spill the beans. Keep it concise, though; we're not writing a novel here. A snapshot of your passions creates instant relatability.

Troubleshooting: "But I have too many passions!" I hear you. Pick the top three, the ones that make you jump out of bed. Your bio is like a highlight reel, not the entire movie.

3. Add a Dash of Emoji Flair
Emojis are the secret sauce of bios. They're like the confetti of the digital world. Sprinkle a few strategically to add color and emotion. Show your fun side, or use them as bullet points for easy reading.

Troubleshooting: "I'm not fluent in Emoji-ese!" No worries, amigo. Start with the basics. A heart, a camera, or a slice of pizza can speak volumes. Soon, you'll be the Shakespeare of smileys.

4. Hashtag Heroics
Got a branded hashtag or a tagline that captures your essence? Slap it in there! Hashtags add a touch of professionalism and help others discover your vibe. #AdventureAwaits or #SushiSorcerer, anyone?

Troubleshooting: "But what if my hashtag is too long?" Short and sweet is the name of the game. If it's a mouthful, consider abbreviating or using an acronym. You want it to be memorable, not a tongue-twister.

Key Takeaways
- Your bio is your chance to be a digital peacock – flaunt those feathers!
- Keep it short, sweet, and true to your awesome self.
- Emojis are your expressive sidekicks; use them wisely.
- Hashtags add flair and help others find their way to your corner of the internet.

Your bio is the welcome mat to your Instagram world. Let it be as inviting as a warm hug. In the next chapter, we'll unravel the mysteries of the contact buttons, making it easy for your fans to slide into your DMs or check out your latest masterpiece. Get ready to bio-ify and beautify!

Choosing the Right Profile Picture

Step 1: Profile Pic Magic
Ah, the mighty profile picture, the face of your Instagram kingdom! Choosing the right one is not just a decision; it's a statement. Get ready to embark on the journey of Profile Pic Magic, where your face becomes the superhero cape of your digital identity.

1. Clarity is Queen
First things first, your face should be the star of the show. Opt for a clear, well-lit photo where your features shine. No one wants to play detective, squinting at a pixelated version of you. Crisp and clear, my friend!

Troubleshooting: "But my camera is potato quality!" Fear not. Natural light works wonders. Find a spot by the window or bask in the glory of golden-hour sunlight. A glow-up awaits!

2. Authenticity Trumps Perfection
Your profile pic is not a Vogue cover shoot – it's a glimpse into the real you. Choose a photo that captures your essence, imperfections and all. Authenticity resonates more than a hundred staged shots.

Troubleshooting: "I can't choose between serious or smiling!" Mix it up! Alternate between a genuine smile and a more composed look. You're a multi-faceted gem, not a one-trick pony.

3. Solo Spotlight or Group Galore?
While friend squads are fantastic, your profile pic is not the place for a Where's Waldo challenge. Ensure you're the main act. If you do opt for a group pic, make sure it's clear who the real star is – that's you!

Troubleshooting: "But my pet iguana is my bestie!" A solo pic is great, but if your pet steals the show, let them shine in your feed. The profile pic, though, should be the face that launched a thousand likes, yours.

4. Cohesiveness with Your Vibe
Your profile pic sets the tone for your entire feed. Whether you're going for a laid-back vibe or channeling your inner superhero, make sure it aligns with your overall Instagram aesthetic. Consistency is the key to a visually stunning profile.

Troubleshooting: "I change my aesthetic like I change socks!" No judgment, my friend. Just ensure your profile pic is a timeless representation of you. Your future self will thank you.

Key Takeaways
- Clarity is crucial; no one likes a blurry detective game.
- Authenticity over perfection – imperfections are the real MVPs.
- Solo or group, make sure the spotlight is on you.
- Ensure your profile pic vibes with your overall aesthetic.

Your profile pic is the ambassador of your Instagram world. Make it a head-turner! In the next chapter, we'll tackle the art of crafting an irresistible bio. Get ready to showcase the real you!

Chapter 2

Crafting Captivating Visual Content

The Power of Visual Storytelling

Welcome to the heart of Instagram enchantment – where pixels weave tales, and images speak volumes. In this chapter, we delve into the magic of Visual Storytelling, transforming your grid into a spellbinding narrative that captivates and enthralls your audience.

1. Painting with Pixels: The Essence of Visual Storytelling
Visual storytelling is the wizardry that turns a mere collection of pictures into a captivating saga. It's not just about pretty snapshots; it's about crafting a cohesive visual journey that invites your audience to step into your world. Each post is a brushstroke, contributing to the masterpiece of your Instagram tale.

Troubleshooting: "But I'm no Van Gogh with a camera!" Fear not, fellow storyteller. It's not about fancy equipment; it's about intention. Even your smartphone can wield magic if you capture moments with purpose.

2. Find Your Theme: Your Story's Signature Scent

What's the fragrance of your story? Whether it's the aroma of adventure, the scent of nostalgia, or the whiff of humor, your theme is the unique scent that lingers in the minds of your followers. Consistency is key – let your theme be the guiding star of your visual narrative.

Troubleshooting: "I love too many things; I can't pick a theme!" No need for commitment phobia here. Your theme can evolve, but having a loose concept helps maintain a sense of cohesion. It's like telling different chapters of the same epic saga.

3. Compose Your Visual Symphony: The Rule of Thirds and Beyond

Ever heard of the Rule of Thirds? It's not a secret society; it's a composition technique. Imagine your image divided into a tic-tac-toe grid, and your subject placed at the intersections. This simple trick can turn a bland photo into a visual masterpiece.

Troubleshooting: "I keep cutting off heads in my photos!" Adjust your framing. Make sure the key elements are within those magical intersections. Heads deserve to be in the picture, not out of it!

4. The Power of Sequence: Creating a Visual Narrative

Your Instagram grid is a scrollable storybook. Consider the flow as you post. Arrange your images to create a narrative, a journey for your audience to embark upon. A cohesive sequence enhances the storytelling experience.

Troubleshooting: "But I'm not a novelist; I just post random stuff!" No worries, storyteller-in-training. Start small. Maybe it's a color scheme or a recurring element. A narrative is just a series of intentional choices.

Key Takeaways
- Visual storytelling turns images into a compelling saga.
- Your theme is the signature scent that makes your story unforgettable.
- Master the Rule of Thirds for visually pleasing compositions.
- Your grid is a scrollable storybook; arrange your posts with intention.

Now, armed with the art of Visual Storytelling, go forth and paint your Instagram canvas with tales that resonate. In the next chapter, we'll unravel the intricacies of crafting a content strategy that keeps your audience eagerly flipping the pages of your visual narrative. Get ready to embark on a journey of storytelling brilliance!

Design Tips for Stunning Posts

Congratulations, maestro of the lens! You've dipped your toes into the magic of visual storytelling, and now it's time to elevate your craft with design prowess. In this chapter, we'll explore the secrets of transforming your snapshots into visually stunning masterpieces that stop the scroll and leave your followers in awe.

1. Embrace the Power of Consistency: Your Visual Signature

Consistency isn't just for breakfast; it's the secret sauce of stunning feeds. Choose a consistent color palette, filter, or editing style that reflects your aesthetic. This visual uniformity creates a harmonious look, turning your grid into a visual wonderland.

Troubleshooting: "But I love all the filters!" Variety is the spice of life, but too much can be overwhelming. Pick a couple of filters that complement your vibe. Consistency doesn't mean monotony.

2. Mind the Negative Space: Less Can Be More

Negative space isn't the enemy; it's the unsung hero of design. Give your visuals room to breathe. Whether it's a minimalist background or a vast sky, negative space enhances focus and adds an air of sophistication to your posts.

Troubleshooting: "But my photos look empty!" Embrace the emptiness. Negative space draws attention to your main subject. It's not absence; it's emphasis.

3. Master the Art of Typography: Words That Wow

Your captions aren't just words; they're design elements. Experiment with fonts and text placement to add flair. A well-designed caption enhances your overall aesthetic and guides your audience through the visual journey.

Troubleshooting: "But I'm not a graphic designer!" No need for a degree in design. Stick to a readable font, play with sizing, and keep it consistent. Soon, you'll be a typography maestro.

4. Play with Symmetry and Patterns: Eye Candy Delight

Symmetry is visually satisfying, and patterns add rhythm to your grid. Experiment with symmetrical compositions or use recurring elements to create a visual dance. It's like orchestrating a symphony with pixels.

Troubleshooting: "I'm not a math whiz; I can't do symmetry!" Fear not, non-mathematician. Symmetry can be as simple as centering your subject. Patterns can be anything repeating, like alternating between selfies and scenic shots.

Key Takeaways
- Consistency in color and editing styles creates a visually harmonious feed.
- Embrace negative space to enhance focus and sophistication.
- Typography is your secret weapon; make your captions visually appealing.
- Experiment with symmetry and patterns for eye-catching visuals.

Armed with these design tips, your posts are poised to be the belle of the Instagram ball. In the next chapter, we'll dive into the nitty-gritty of crafting a content strategy that keeps your audience hungry for more. Get ready to take your visual game to the next level!

Utilizing Instagram's Features (Stories, Reels, IGTV)

Ahoy, fearless content creator! Now that you've mastered the art of visual storytelling and design finesse, it's time to wield the full arsenal of Instagram's magical features. In this chapter, we'll explore how to unleash the power of Stories, Reels, and IGTV, turning your profile into a dynamic, ever-evolving spectacle.

1. Stories: The Fleeting Charms of Ephemeral Content
Stories are like shooting stars in the Instagram galaxy – captivating but fleeting. Use them to share behind-the-scenes glimpses, quick updates, or spontaneous bursts of creativity. With features like polls, questions, and quizzes, turn your Stories into interactive adventures that engage your audience.

Troubleshooting: "But my life is boring!" Nonsense! Even the mundane becomes magical with a creative twist. Share your morning coffee routine, ask for opinions on your outfit, or host a mini Q&A. Spice it up!

2. Reels: The Short and Snappy Showstoppers
Enter the world of Reels, where short-form videos steal the spotlight. Embrace the art of storytelling in 15 to 30 seconds. Whether it's a dance-off, a quick tutorial, or a

comedic skit, Reels are your ticket to capturing attention in a fast-paced world.

Troubleshooting: "I'm not a dancer or a comedian!" You don't need to be. Showcase your talents, share quick tips, or simply tell a micro-story. It's less about perfection and more about authenticity.

3. IGTV: Your Mini Cinematic Universe
IGTV is your very own film festival. Share longer-form content, from tutorials to vlogs, turning your profile into a mini-cinematic universe. IGTV allows your audience to dive deeper into your world, fostering a more profound connection.

Troubleshooting: "But I'm not Spielberg!" No need for a blockbuster budget. IGTV is about authentic, relatable content. Share your passions, experiences, or expertise in a longer format.

4. Cross-Promotion Brilliance: Weaving a Seamless Tapestry
Integrate these features seamlessly. Share a sneak peek of your Reel in Stories, direct your audience to IGTV for the full scoop, and vice versa. Cross-promotion enhances engagement and ensures your audience gets the full experience.

Troubleshooting: "It's like juggling; I might drop the ball!" Practice makes perfect. Experiment with cross-promotion, and soon you'll be juggling like a pro. Your audience will appreciate the variety.

Key Takeaways
- Stories offer ephemeral, interactive snapshots into your life.
- Reels provide short-form, attention-grabbing content.
- IGTV is your platform for longer, immersive storytelling.
- Cross-promotion weaves a cohesive narrative across features.

Now, armed with the knowledge of Instagram's dynamic features, your content will dance, dazzle, and leave your audience craving more. In the next chapter, we'll delve into the art of crafting a content strategy that combines all these elements seamlessly. Get ready to shine on the Instagram stage!

Chapter 3

Developing a Content Strategy

Identifying Your Target Audience

Greetings, strategist extraordinaire! Now that you've painted visual masterpieces and tapped into Instagram's enchanted features, it's time to tailor your content strategy. In this chapter, we embark on the first crucial step: Identifying Your Target Audience. After all, knowing your audience is like having a treasure map, it leads to engagement gold.

1. Define Your Tribe: Who Are Your People?
Begin by asking yourself: Who would vibe with your content? Are you a fitness guru inspiring fellow workout warriors, a foodie delighting taste buds, or a pet enthusiast sharing the adorable antics of your furry companions? Define your tribe based on your passions and expertise.

Troubleshooting: "But my interests are all over the place!" No worries; diversity is the spice of life. Identify the common thread. Your tribe may be as eclectic as your taste in music, and that's the beauty of it.

2. Create Your Ideal Audience Avatar: The Imaginary BFF

Craft a detailed profile of your ideal follower – your content's biggest fan. What are their interests, challenges, and aspirations? This imaginary BFF represents your target audience. Knowing them intimately guides your content decisions.

Troubleshooting: "I feel like I'm creating a character for a novel!" Spot on! Think of it as developing a character in your very own content narrative. This character represents the heart and soul of your audience.

3. Leverage Instagram Insights: The Crystal Ball

Instagram Insights is your content crystal ball. Dive into analytics to understand who interacts with your content. Discover their demographics, location, and when they're most active. This data unveils patterns and preferences, helping you refine your strategy.

Troubleshooting: "Analytics scare me!" Fear not, brave explorer. Start small. Focus on basic metrics like engagement and follower demographics. Over time, you'll navigate the analytics terrain with ease.

4. Engage and Listen: A Two-Way Street

Engagement is a conversation, not a monologue. Actively respond to comments, DMs, and participate in conversations within your niche. Your audience's feedback is a goldmine. Listen to their needs, desires, and challenges, it's the key to content that resonates.

Troubleshooting: "I feel like I'm talking to an empty room!" Rome wasn't built in a day, nor was an engaged audience. Consistency is key. Keep the conversation flowing, and your room will fill up.

Key Takeaways
- Define your tribe based on your passions and expertise.
- Craft an ideal audience avatar to guide your content decisions.
- Leverage Instagram Insights for valuable data and trends.
- Engagement is a two-way street, listen, respond, and adapt.

Identifying your target audience is the compass that guides your content ship. In the next chapter, we'll explore the importance of planning a consistent posting schedule. Get ready to set sail into the seas of strategic content creation!

Planning a Consistent Posting Schedule

Ahoy, Captain of Content Calendars! Now that you've identified your audience, it's time to set sail on the seas of consistency. In this chapter, we'll unravel the importance of Planning a Consistent Posting Schedule, the wind in your content sails that keeps your audience aboard and eagerly awaiting your next adventure.

1. Choose Your Posting Frequency: Set Sail with Intent
Consider your audience's appetite and your capacity. Are you a daily diarist, a weekly wordsmith, or a monthly maestro? Choose a posting frequency that aligns with your content creation capabilities and keeps your audience engaged without overwhelming them.

Troubleshooting: "I'm drowning in content creation!" Quality over quantity, my friend. If daily feels like a storm, navigate to a schedule that allows you to create exceptional content consistently.

2. Pick Optimal Posting Times: Synchronize with Your Audience
Instagram Insights and analytics are your compass here. Identify when your audience is most active. Are they early morning risers, lunchtime scrollers, or night owls? Timing your posts when your audience is online increases visibility and engagement.

Troubleshooting: "But I have a global audience!" Aha, time zones, the navigational challenge of the digital world. Experiment with posting at different times to find the sweet spot for maximum engagement.

3. Craft a Content Calendar: Plot Your Course
A content calendar is your treasure map for consistent posting. Plan your posts in advance, considering themes, promotions, and relevant events. This proactive approach ensures a steady flow of content, preventing last-minute scrambles.

Troubleshooting: "I'm not a planner; I'm a spontaneous creator!" Spontaneity is a gift, but a content calendar is your safety net. It doesn't stifle creativity; it ensures your brilliance is shared consistently.

4. Diversify Your Content: Keep the Seas Interesting
Variety is the spice of Instagram life. Mix up your content types, photos, videos, stories, and reels. A diverse content menu keeps your audience engaged and eagerly anticipating your next creation.

Troubleshooting: "I'm stuck in a content rut!" Fear not, content explorer. Spice up your feed with different formats, behind-the-scenes glimpses, or user-generated content. Shake it like a content cocktail.

Key Takeaways
- Choose a posting frequency that aligns with your capacity.
- Time your posts for optimal audience engagement.
- Craft a content calendar to plan ahead and maintain consistency.
- Diversify your content to keep your audience engaged.

Consistency is the anchor that stabilizes your content ship. In the next chapter, we'll delve into the art of balancing content variety for maximum engagement. Get ready to hoist the sails of creativity and set course for a captivating content journey!

Balancing Content Variety for Engagement

Hello, Maestro of Variety! Now that you've set sail with a consistent posting schedule, it's time to steer your content ship through the seas of diversity. In this chapter, we'll uncover the secrets of Balancing Content Variety for Engagement, because a dynamic feed is a captivating feed.

1. Mix and Match Content Types: The Content Buffet
Variety is not just the spice of life; it's the heartbeat of your Instagram feed. Mix static posts with dynamic content like videos, stories, and reels. Offer your audience a buffet of content experiences, ensuring there's something for every taste.

Troubleshooting: "But I'm a photo aficionado!" No worries, Ansel Adams. Integrate short videos or share your creative process in Stories. The key is not to abandon your forte but to expand your content palette.

2. Themes and Series: Consistency in Diversity
Inject consistency into diversity by incorporating themes or series. Whether it's a weekly #ThrowbackThursday, a monthly Q&A, or a themed photo challenge, these recurring elements create anticipation and engagement.

Troubleshooting: "I fear commitment to themes!" Themes are flexible. It could be as simple as a recurring color, mood, or subject. Consistency doesn't mean monotony; it means reliability.

3. Behind-the-Scenes Glimpses: The Human Touch
Peek behind the curtain and let your audience see the wizardry behind your content. Share behind-the-scenes glimpses, bloopers, or a day in your life. Humanizing your content builds a connection and adds authenticity.

Troubleshooting: "But my life is mundane!" The mundane is the relatable goldmine. Share the chaos of your workspace, the mishaps of your creative process, or the joy in the small, everyday moments.

4. User-Generated Content: The Community Collaborative
Turn your audience into co-creators by incorporating user-generated content. Encourage followers to share their experiences with your products, recreate your recipes, or showcase their interpretations of your challenges. It fosters a sense of community and participation.

Troubleshooting: "What if nobody participates?" Plant the seeds by initiating the first few challenges. Showcase them and watch the ripple effect. People love to be part of something bigger.

Key Takeaways
- Mix content types for a dynamic feed experience.
- Integrate recurring themes or series for consistency.
- Share behind-the-scenes moments for authenticity.
- Engage your community with user-generated content.

Balancing content variety is the compass that navigates your audience through a diverse, engaging landscape. In the next chapter, we'll delve into the mysterious world of mastering hashtags. Brace yourself for a journey through the hashtag galaxy!

It's time to steer your content ship through the seas of diversity.

Chapter 4

Mastering Hashtags

Understanding the Role of Hashtags

Greetings, Hashtag Explorer! As you navigate the vast sea of Instagram, understanding the power and purpose of hashtags is like wielding a magic wand. In this chapter, we'll delve into the art of Mastering Hashtags – the secret sauce to amplify your content's reach and beckon the right audience to your digital shores.

1. Decoding the Hashtag Language: #WhatOnEarthIsThis?
Hashtags are not alien hieroglyphs; they're your content's tour guides. These clickable keywords categorize your posts and connect them to broader conversations. Whether it's #TravelTuesday or #DIYProjects, hashtags open doors to wider audiences searching for specific content.

Troubleshooting: "But there are so many! Which ones do I use?" Start with relevance. Choose hashtags that directly relate to your content. Mix popular ones with niche-specific tags for a balanced approach.

2. The Art of Research: #SeekAndYouShallFind

Research is your hashtag compass. Explore what hashtags your audience and competitors use. Dive into the analytics of similar posts and identify trending hashtags. Strategic research ensures you're riding the waves of current conversations.

Troubleshooting: "Research sounds tedious!" It's an investment, not a chore. Use Instagram's search bar, explore related posts, and discover trending tags. Soon, you'll be hashtag Sherlock.

3. Size Matters: Balancing Popularity and Specificity

Hashtags come in all sizes, from giants with millions of uses to tiny gems with a dedicated few. Strive for a mix. Popular hashtags cast a wide net, while niche ones target a specific audience. A balanced approach maximizes visibility and engagement.

Troubleshooting: "My posts drown in popular hashtags!" Be the big fish in a small pond. Mix in niche hashtags relevant to your content. It's about finding the sweet spot where your content stands out.

4. Crafting Branded Hashtags: #ClaimYourTerritory

Leave your mark on the Instagram landscape with a branded hashtag. It could be your name, catchphrase, or a unique tag related to your brand. Branded hashtags create a digital fingerprint, making it easier for your audience to find and engage with your content.

Troubleshooting: "But what if nobody uses it?" Kickstart the trend yourself. Encourage your audience to use your branded hashtag, and showcase their posts. It's a collaborative effort that turns your hashtag into a community symbol.

Key Takeaways
- Hashtags categorize and connect your content to broader conversations.
- Research trending and relevant hashtags for strategic use.
- Balance popular and niche hashtags for optimal reach.
- Create and promote branded hashtags for community engagement.

Researching and Choosing Effective Hashtags

Ahoy, Hashtag Archaeologist! In this chapter, we'll embark on a thrilling expedition through the dense jungle of hashtags, learning the art of Researching and Choosing Effective Hashtags. Buckle up, because we're diving deep into the hashtag terrain to uncover the hidden treasures that will boost your content's discoverability.

1. Survey the Landscape: What's Trending?
Before you set sail, survey the hashtag landscape. Explore what's trending in your niche and industry. Instagram's search bar is your compass – type in relevant keywords and discover the popularity and frequency of related hashtags.

Troubleshooting: "I'm lost in the jungle of hashtags!" Start small. Begin with broad topics and gradually narrow down to more specific ones. Observe which hashtags resonate with your audience and competitors.

2. Competitor Analysis: Learn from the Natives
Your competitors are the seasoned explorers of the hashtag jungle. Analyze their posts to identify the hashtags they use. This not only gives you insights into

effective hashtags but also helps you understand your shared audience and industry trends.

Troubleshooting: "But won't that make me a copycat?" Far from it! It's about learning and adapting. Identify common hashtags and then add your unique twist. Your posts should stand out while still being part of the conversation.

3. Mix of Size and Specificity: The Goldilocks Principle
When selecting hashtags, embrace the Goldilocks principle, not too big, not too small, just right. Mix popular, broad hashtags with niche, specific ones. This balanced approach ensures your content reaches a broad audience while connecting with those deeply interested in your niche.

Troubleshooting: "But how do I know which size is right?" Experimentation is your guide. Monitor the performance of your posts with different-sized hashtags. Over time, you'll discover the sweet spot for your content.

4. Create Your Arsenal: Branded and Community Hashtags
Arm yourself with a powerful arsenal of hashtags. Develop a combination that includes:

Branded Hashtags: Unique to your brand.
Community Hashtags: Widely used by your audience.
Industry-specific Hashtags: Relevant to your niche.

This diverse collection ensures your content aligns with broader conversations, your brand identity, and the interests of your community.

Troubleshooting: "I'm overwhelmed by hashtag choices!" Keep it simple. Start with a core set of hashtags that cover different aspects – brand, community, and industry. As you gain confidence, you can expand your arsenal.

Key Takeaways
- Survey the hashtag landscape to identify trends.
- Analyze competitor posts for effective hashtag insights.
- Balance popular and niche hashtags for optimal reach.
- Create a diverse arsenal with branded, community, and industry-specific hashtags.

Armed with effective hashtags, your content is equipped for a successful expedition through the Instagram wilderness.!

Creating Your Own Branded Hashtag

Ahoy, Brand Maverick! In this chapter, we'll embark on the exciting journey of Creating Your Own Branded Hashtag, the digital flag that marks your territory in the vast landscape of social media. Ready to craft a hashtag that becomes synonymous with your brand? Let's dive in!

1. Reflect Your Brand Identity: The Hashtag Mirror
Your branded hashtag is more than a symbol; it's a reflection of your brand's essence. Consider your brand's personality, values, and mission. Whether it's playful, empowering, or educational, your hashtag should resonate with your audience and mirror your brand identity.

Troubleshooting: "I'm not sure how to reflect my brand!" Start with keywords that encapsulate your brand's vibe. Play around with combinations until you find one that feels like a perfect match.

2. Keep it Memorable and Simple: #LessIsMore
A memorable hashtag is like an earworm, once heard, it sticks. Keep it simple, avoiding complex words or obscure references. It should be easy to spell, pronounce, and recall. Think of it as a concise tagline that encapsulates your brand's message.

Troubleshooting: "But everything feels too generic!" Embrace simplicity. Think about Nike's #JustDoIt short, memorable, and instantly associated with the brand. Your hashtag can have the same impact.

3. Unique and Unambiguous: The Digital Snowflake

Your branded hashtag is your digital snowflake, one of a kind. Ensure it's not in use by others and is distinctive to your brand. Avoid generic terms that may get lost in a sea of similar hashtags. Uniqueness ensures your hashtag stands out in the crowd.

Troubleshooting: "What if someone else is already using it?" Tweak and customize. Add your brand name, initials, or a relevant term to make it unique. Remember, your hashtag is like a digital signature.

4. Promote and Encourage Use: #SpreadTheWord

A hashtag's power lies in its usage. Actively promote your branded hashtag across your social media channels, encouraging followers to incorporate it in their posts. Showcase user-generated content with your hashtag, turning it into a community symbol.

Troubleshooting: "But what if no one uses it?" Kickstart the trend yourself. Integrate it into your posts, stories, and captions. Host challenges or contests tied to your hashtag. The more you promote, the more likely your audience will join in.

Key Takeaways
- Reflect your brand identity in your hashtag.
- Keep your branded hashtag memorable and simple.
- Ensure your hashtag is unique and unambiguous.
- Actively promote and encourage the use of your branded hashtag.

Your branded hashtag is the beacon that guides your community back to your brand. In the next chapter, we'll explore the dynamic world of engaging with your audience. Get ready to dive into the sea of comments, likes, and direct messages!

Chapter 5

Leveraging Influencer Collaborations

Finding and Connecting with Relevant Influencers

Greetings, Collaborator Extraordinaire! In this chapter, we embark on the thrilling journey of Leveraging Influencer Collaborations. The key to a successful collaboration lies in finding and connecting with influencers who align seamlessly with your brand. Let's unravel the art of identifying the right influencers and establishing meaningful connections.

1. Define Your Ideal Influencer: The Perfect Dance Partner
Before diving into the vast sea of influencers, define the qualities of your ideal collaborator. Consider factors like audience demographics, values, and content style. Your perfect dance partner should resonate with your brand and seamlessly integrate into your community.

Troubleshooting: "What if I can't find the perfect fit?" Flexibility is key. Prioritize alignment in terms of values and audience, and be open to influencers who bring their unique flair to the collaboration.

2. Explore Relevant Niches: The Influencer Ecosystem
Influencers are diverse, each occupying their unique niche. Explore various niches relevant to your brand. If you're in the fitness industry, look beyond general fitness influencers to find those specializing in specific areas like yoga, HIIT, or nutrition. The influencer ecosystem is rich, venture into its various habitats.

Troubleshooting: I'm overwhelmed by the options!" Narrow down your focus. Identify niches that directly connect with your audience. Quality trumps quantity; a smaller, engaged audience often yields better results.

3. Social Media Stalking (Ethically): The Research Ballet
Engage in some ethical social media stalking to understand potential collaborators better. Dive into their content, engagement rates, and audience interactions. This research ballet helps ensure their values align with yours, and they genuinely connect with their followers.

Troubleshooting: "Feels like spying!" Think of it as getting to know someone before extending an invitation.

Look for authenticity, engagement, and a genuine connection with their audience.

4. Utilize Influencer Platforms: The Digital Matchmaker

In the age of technology, influencer platforms act as digital matchmakers. Platforms like AspireIQ, Traackr, or Influence.co connect brands with influencers based on specific criteria. Utilize these tools to streamline your search and discover potential collaborators efficiently.

Troubleshooting: "I prefer a personal touch!" Platforms are tools, not replacements. Use them to discover influencers, but always follow up with personal research to ensure compatibility.

Key Takeaways
- Clearly define the qualities of your ideal influencer collaborator.
- Explore diverse niches within the influencer ecosystem.
- Ethically research potential collaborators' content and engagement.
- Utilize influencer platforms as a digital matchmaking tool.

Armed with the knowledge of finding and connecting with influencers, you're ready to curate impactful collaborations. In the next chapter, we'll delve into the art of creating compelling content with your newfound influencer allies. Get ready for a creative partnership like no other!

Negotiating Effective Collaborations

Ahoy, Negotiation Maestro! In the realm of influencer collaborations, successful negotiations are the compass that steers your ship toward mutual benefit. In this chapter, we'll dive into the art of Negotiating Effective Collaborations, ensuring a harmonious partnership that resonates with both parties.

1. Clarify Expectations: Setting Sail with Transparency
Before diving into negotiations, embark on a journey of clarity. Clearly define the expectations, deliverables, and goals for the collaboration. Discuss content formats, posting schedules, and the overall narrative you want to weave together. Transparency at this stage is your anchor for a smooth voyage.

Troubleshooting: "What if we have different expectations?" It's normal to have variations. Discuss and find common ground. Be open to compromise, ensuring both parties feel heard and valued.

2. Know Your Budget: The Financial Map
Navigate the financial waters with a clear budget in mind. Determine the value of the collaboration and what you're willing to invest. Be realistic about your financial capacity and consider the influencer's rates. A

transparent conversation about compensation ensures a fair and respectful negotiation.

Troubleshooting: "But I'm on a tight budget!" Quality over quantity. If finances are limited, consider smaller influencers or explore alternative compensation methods, such as product exchange or shared promotional efforts.

3. Co-create the Narrative: A Storytelling Partnership
Influencers are storytellers, and your collaboration is a joint narrative. Discuss the storytelling elements, the key messages you want to convey, and how the influencer's unique voice can enhance the story. This collaborative approach ensures an authentic and engaging narrative.

Troubleshooting: "I want creative control!" Balance is key. While it's essential to guide the narrative, give influencers creative freedom. Trust their expertise in connecting with their audience.

4. Measureable Metrics: Charting the Success Course
Before sealing the deal, agree on measurable metrics to gauge the collaboration's success. Whether it's engagement rates, click-throughs, or brand mentions, having clear metrics helps both parties assess the impact. A successful collaboration is one where both the brand and influencer achieve their objectives.

Troubleshooting: "What if the metrics don't meet expectations?" Learn and adapt. Use the insights gained to refine future collaborations. It's a journey of continuous improvement.

Key Takeaways
- Clearly define expectations, deliverables, and goals.
- Determine a realistic budget and be transparent about compensation.
- Co-create the narrative for an authentic storytelling partnership.
- Establish measurable metrics to gauge collaboration success.

Armed with effective negotiation skills, your influencer collaborations are poised for success. In the next chapter, we'll explore the dynamic world of measuring and analyzing the impact of your collaborations. Get ready to set sail into the seas of influencer collaboration analytics!

Maximizing the Impact of Influencer Partnerships

Hello, Impact Architect! Now that you've navigated the negotiation seas, it's time to unleash the full potential of your influencer partnerships. In this chapter, we'll explore strategies for Maximizing the Impact of Influencer Collaborations, ensuring your brand message resonates far and wide.

1. Authenticity is King: Let Influencers Be Themselves
The heart of any impactful collaboration is authenticity. Allow influencers the creative freedom to infuse their unique voice into the content. When influencers authentically engage with your brand, their audience is more likely to trust and resonate with your message.

Enhancement Tip: Encourage influencers to share personal anecdotes or experiences related to your product or service. Authenticity is a magnet for audience connection.

2. Leverage Multi-Platform Presence: Expanding Horizons
Influencers are digital nomads, roaming across various platforms. Capitalize on their multi-platform presence to reach diverse audiences. If an influencer is renowned on Instagram, explore collaborations on YouTube, Twitter,

or even TikTok. Diversify the landscape for maximum impact.

Enhancement Tip: Cross-promote the collaboration across platforms, directing each audience to explore the full content spectrum. It's a digital tour de force.

3. Interactive Campaigns: Turning Audiences into Participants

Transform passive viewers into active participants by incorporating interactive elements. Whether it's a Q&A session, a challenge, or a giveaway, interactive campaigns boost engagement. Influencers become conduits for two-way communication, fostering a sense of community.

Enhancement Tip: Create branded hashtags for the campaign, encouraging audiences to join the conversation. It's a dynamic way to track engagement and build a collaborative narrative.

4. Track and Analyze: The Data Compass

Measure the ripples of your collaboration by diligently tracking and analyzing data. Monitor engagement rates, click-throughs, and audience demographics. Leverage analytics tools to gain insights into what worked well and areas for improvement. Data is the compass guiding future impactful collaborations.

Enhancement Tip: Collaborate with influencers to gather their insights. They often have a deep understanding of their audience's preferences and can provide valuable feedback.

Key Takeaways
- Prioritize authenticity to build trust with the influencer's audience.
- Leverage influencers' presence across multiple platforms for broader reach.
- Incorporate interactive elements to turn audiences into active participants.
- Track and analyze data to measure the impact and refine future collaborations.

Maximizing the impact of influencer partnerships is an ongoing journey of refinement and innovation. In the next chapter, we'll explore the ever-evolving landscape of viral trends and how to ride the waves of digital phenomena. Get ready for a thrilling adventure into the world of online virality!

Chapter 6

Riding the Wave of Viral Trends

Identifying and Participating in Viral Challenges

Hello, Trend Surfer! In this chapter, we'll dive into the exhilarating world of viral trends, where the tides of digital phenomena shape the landscape of social media. Buckle up as we explore the art of Identifying and Participating in Viral Challenges, ensuring you ride the wave of online trends like a seasoned surfer.

1. Stay Vigilant: The Trend Watchtower
The first rule of catching a wave is to spot it from afar. Stay vigilant by keeping a keen eye on social media platforms. Monitor popular hashtags, explore trending topics, and be attuned to the conversations buzzing across the digital realm. The trend watchtower is your vantage point for spotting the next big wave.

Surfing Tip: Set up notifications for trending hashtags and regularly explore the 'Explore' or 'Discover' sections on platforms like Instagram and TikTok.

2. Understand the Mechanics: Decoding Viral Alchemy
Viral challenges have a secret sauce, understand the mechanics, and you unlock the alchemy. Analyze past challenges to identify common elements, the engaging hooks, simplicity, and inclusivity that encourage mass participation. Decoding the viral formula is your key to crafting a challenge that resonates.

Surfing Tip: Dive into the history of viral challenges. What made them click? How did they encourage participation? Learn from the success stories.

3. Create Engaging Content: The Viral Bait
Participation in a viral challenge requires compelling content. Craft visually appealing, shareable, and easily replicable content that aligns with the challenge theme. The goal is to create a ripple effect – one person participates, and their followers catch the wave, turning it into a digital cascade.

Surfing Tip: Infuse creativity into your content. Whether it's a dance, a lip-sync, or a unique twist, make your participation stand out in the crowd.

4. Leverage Cross-Platform Appeal: The Wave Expander

A true viral wave knows no bounds. Extend your challenge's reach by leveraging cross-platform appeal. Encourage participants to share their entries on various platforms, ensuring the wave transcends boundaries and resonates with diverse audiences.

Surfing Tip: Tailor your challenge to suit different platforms. What works on TikTok might need a slight adjustment for Instagram or Twitter. Adaptability ensures maximum impact.

Key Takeaways
- Stay vigilant by actively monitoring social media for emerging trends.
- Understand the mechanics of past viral challenges to decode the formula.
- Create engaging and shareable content that aligns with the challenge theme.
- Leverage cross-platform appeal to expand the reach of your viral challenge.

Capitalizing on Trending Topics

Hey Trend Trailblazer! In this chapter, we're setting sail into the dynamic realm of capitalizing on trending topics. Whether it's a viral challenge, a hashtag campaign, or a hot discussion, strategically embracing what's trending can propel your brand into the spotlight. Let's dive in and unlock the secrets of Capitalizing on Trending Topics.

1. Listen and Learn: The Trending Symphony
The first note in the trending symphony is listening. Stay tuned to social media platforms, industry news, and relevant forums. Pay attention to conversations, emerging hashtags, and popular discussions. The digital landscape is a dynamic stage, and your ability to listen sets the tone for successful participation.

Strategic Tip: Set up social listening tools to stay informed about real-time trends and discussions related to your industry or niche.

2. Align with Your Brand Voice: The Trend Harmony
Not every trend is a melody suited for your brand, and that's okay. Choose trends that align with your brand voice, values, and target audience. The goal is not just to ride the wave but to create a harmonious resonance that strengthens your brand identity.

Strategic Tip: Before jumping on a trend, ask: Does this align with our brand message? Will our audience resonate with this content?

3. Act Swiftly: The Trend Tempo
Trends have a tempo, a rhythm that demands swift action. Once you identify a relevant trend, act promptly. Create content, craft responses, or join discussions in a timely manner. The faster your response, the higher your chances of being part of the trending conversation.

Strategic Tip: Have a streamlined approval process in place. Swift action often requires quick decision-making, so minimize bureaucratic delays.

4. Engage Authentically: The Trend Conversation
Engaging with trending topics goes beyond riding the wave; it's about contributing authentically to the conversation. Craft content or responses that add value, spark discussions, or bring a unique perspective. Authentic engagement is the catalyst for meaningful connections.

Strategic Tip: Encourage your audience to share their thoughts on the trending topic. User-generated content adds authenticity and widens the conversation.

Key Takeaways
- Listen actively to stay informed about trending topics.
- Align with trends that resonate with your brand voice and audience.
- Act swiftly to create timely and relevant content.
- Engage authentically to contribute meaningfully to the trend conversation.

By strategically capitalizing on trending topics, you position your brand as agile, relevant, and actively engaged in the digital discourse. In the next chapter, we'll explore the art of crafting visually stunning posts that captivate your audience. Get ready to unleash the power of visual storytelling!

Staying Authentic While Riding Trends

Hello, Authentic Voyager! In the exhilarating journey of capitalizing on trends, staying true to your brand's authenticity is your compass. In this chapter, we'll navigate the waters of trend-surfing while keeping the sails of authenticity unfurled. Let's dive into the art of Staying Authentic While Riding Trends.

1. Know Your Brand Values: The North Star
Authenticity begins with a deep understanding of your brand values. These values are your guiding North Star in the vast ocean of trends. Before embracing a trend, ensure it aligns with the principles and beliefs that define your brand.

Authenticity Anchor: Create a list of core values that represent your brand identity. Use it as a litmus test when evaluating trends.

2. Add Your Unique Flavor: The Authentic Spice Rack
Trends are like ingredients, and your brand is the chef. Don't be afraid to add your unique flavor to the mix. Whether it's a trending hashtag, challenge, or topic, infuse it with your brand's personality. This not only distinguishes your content but also maintains a consistent taste across your brand.

Authenticity Spice Tip: Before participating in a trend, brainstorm ways to incorporate elements that reflect your brand's tone, style, or humor.

3. Be Selective: The Authentic Gatekeeper
Not every trend is a suitable ride for your brand. Be discerning. Choose trends that not only align with your values but also provide an opportunity for meaningful engagement with your audience. Authenticity thrives in the space where genuine connection happens.

Authenticity Gatekeeper Rule: Ask yourself, "Does this trend genuinely resonate with our audience, or are we just following the crowd?"

4. Transparent Communication: The Authentic Dialogue
When participating in a trend, communicate transparently with your audience. Share why you're joining the conversation, how it aligns with your brand, and invite their thoughts. Transparent communication builds trust and ensures your audience understands the genuine intention behind your participation.

Authenticity Dialogue Tip: Craft captions or statements that explain your connection to the trend. Share behind-the-scenes insights to humanize your engagement.

Key Takeaways
- Anchor your trend participation in your brand's core values.
- Infuse trends with your brand's unique personality.
- Be selective, choosing trends that align with your values and engage your audience.
- Communicate transparently to build trust with your audience.

Staying authentic while riding trends is a delicate dance, but with your brand values as a guide, you can navigate the trend waters gracefully. In the next chapter, we'll delve into the nuts and bolts of crafting visually stunning posts. Get ready to elevate your visual storytelling game!

Chapter 7

Engaging with Your Audience

Responding to Comments and Direct Messages

Greetings, Conversation Maestro! In this chapter, we're delving into the art of Engaging with Your Audience by exploring the nuances of responding to comments and direct messages. These digital conversations are the heartbeat of your online community, and mastering the art of engagement ensures a harmonious and thriving relationship with your audience.

1. Timely Responses: The Prompt Orchestra
In the symphony of social media, timing is everything. Respond promptly to comments and direct messages to keep the conversation flowing. Your audience will appreciate the real-time interaction, creating a dynamic and engaging dialogue.

Engagement Maestro Tip: Set aside dedicated time for engagement, and consider turning on notifications for immediate responses to urgent inquiries or comments.

2. Personalized Touch: The Tailored Serenade
Tailor your responses to add a personalized touch. Address your audience by name if possible, acknowledge their specific comments, and express genuine appreciation. A personalized response transforms a generic interaction into a memorable exchange.

Engagement Maestro Tip: Use emojis and casual language to inject warmth and personality into your responses, creating a more intimate connection.

3. Encourage Further Interaction: The Open Invitation
Transform one-time interactions into ongoing conversations by encouraging further engagement. Pose questions, seek opinions, or invite your audience to share their experiences. This not only deepens your connection but also turns your social platforms into vibrant communities.

Engagement Maestro Tip: Conclude responses with open-ended questions to invite more comments and foster a sense of community participation.

4. Handle Feedback Gracefully: The Constructive Dance

Not all interactions are sunshine and rainbows. Embrace both positive and constructive feedback gracefully. Respond with empathy, acknowledge concerns, and demonstrate your commitment to continuous improvement. Turning challenges into opportunities showcases your dedication to your audience.

Engagement Maestro Tip: Respond to criticism with a positive attitude. Share how you plan to address concerns, reinforcing your commitment to providing value.

Key Takeaways
- Respond promptly to comments and direct messages for real-time engagement.
- Add a personalized touch to your responses for a more intimate connection.
- Encourage further interaction by posing questions and inviting opinions.
- Handle feedback gracefully, turning challenges into opportunities for improvement.

Running Contests and Giveaways

Hello, Engagement Architect! In this chapter, we're diving into the exciting world of Running Contests and Giveaways, a powerful strategy to captivate your audience, boost interaction, and spread the joy. Let's unlock the secrets of orchestrating contests that not only excite your community but also elevate your brand engagement.

1. Define Clear Objectives: The Contest Blueprint
Before launching a contest or giveaway, define clear objectives. Whether it's increasing brand visibility, growing your follower count, or promoting a new product, having a well-defined purpose guides the structure and rules of your contest.

Contest Architect Tip: Align your objectives with your overall marketing strategy to ensure a seamless integration of the contest into your brand narrative.

2. Choose the Right Platform: The Engagement Stage
Select a platform that aligns with your audience's preferences and behavior. Whether it's Instagram, Twitter, or a dedicated landing page on your website, choose the stage where your community is most active. Each platform has its unique dynamics, so tailor your contest to suit the chosen space.

Contest Architect Tip: Leverage the features of the chosen platform. For Instagram, consider visually appealing posts and stories; for Twitter, focus on concise and engaging tweets.

3. Craft Irresistible Prizes: The Gift Symphony
Prizes are the heartbeat of your contest, make them irresistible. Consider prizes that resonate with your audience's interests and preferences. Whether it's exclusive products, experiences, or collaborations, the allure of the prize enhances participation.

Contest Architect Tip: Ensure the prizes align with your brand, creating a natural connection between the contest and your overall identity.

4. Simple Participation Rules: The Accessibility Dance
Keep participation rules simple and accessible. Complicated rules can deter potential participants. Whether it's tagging friends, sharing posts, or answering questions, make the entry process straightforward and enjoyable.

Contest Architect Tip: Clearly communicate the rules and steps for participation. Use visual aids, such as infographics or step-by-step guides, to enhance clarity.

5. Build Anticipation: The Buzz Crescendo

Create a buzz leading up to the contest launch. Tease your audience with sneak peeks, countdowns, or behind-the-scenes content. Building anticipation generates excitement and ensures a robust initial response when the contest officially kicks off.

Contest Architect Tip: Utilize storytelling techniques to create a narrative around the contest. Share anecdotes, testimonials, or previews to build intrigue.

6. Engage Throughout: The Community Connection

Don't let engagement fizzle after the contest launch. Stay actively involved throughout the contest duration. Respond to comments, encourage participant interactions, and showcase the progress of the contest. Active engagement sustains the excitement.

Contest Architect Tip: Create a dedicated hashtag for the contest to aggregate entries and foster a sense of community around the event.

Key Takeaways
- Define clear objectives to guide the structure and rules of your contest.
- Choose the right platform based on your audience's preferences.

- Craft irresistible prizes that align with your brand identity.
- Keep participation rules simple and accessible for a wider audience.
- Build anticipation leading up to the contest launch.
- Stay actively engaged throughout the contest to sustain excitement.

Hosting Live Q&A Sessions and Polls

Greetings, Interaction Maestro! In this chapter, we'll explore the captivating world of Hosting Live Q&A Sessions and Polls, a dynamic duo that not only enhances audience engagement but also creates a real-time dialogue between you and your community. Let's dive into the art of interactive sessions that bring your brand to life.

1. Live Q&A Sessions: The Personal Connection
The Stage is Set: Choose a platform suitable for live sessions, such as Instagram Live, Facebook Live, or YouTube Live. Announce the session in advance to build anticipation.

Open the Floor: Begin the session by welcoming participants and encouraging them to submit questions. Create a mix of pre-prepared questions and live queries to keep the session dynamic.

Personal Touch: Address participants by name when responding to their questions. Share personal anecdotes, stories, or behind-the-scenes insights to humanize the interaction.

Engagement Boost: Encourage real-time interaction by responding to comments and reactions during the session. Foster a sense of community by acknowledging your audience.

2. Live Polls: The Instant Feedback Loop

Interactive Decision-Making: Integrate live polls into your sessions to foster participation and gather instant feedback. Pose questions related to your brand, products, or upcoming initiatives.

Create a Narrative: Craft polls that tell a story or guide the session's direction. Whether it's choosing between product options or deciding the next topic to discuss, polls add an interactive layer.

Real-Time Results: Share poll results immediately, creating a sense of excitement and involvement. Discuss the outcomes, and use them as a springboard for further conversation.

Audience Empowerment: Empower your audience by allowing them to shape certain aspects of your content or decisions. This not only engages them but also makes them feel valued.

3. Promote and Prepare: The Pre-Event Overture

Build Anticipation: Announce your live session and polls in advance across your social media channels.

Tease the topics you'll cover or the questions you'll ask. Create visual assets to generate buzz.

Prepare Engaging Content: Plan and prepare content that complements your live session. Whether it's slides, visuals, or demos, ensure your presentation is visually appealing and aligns with your brand.

Encourage Participation: Encourage your audience to submit questions or suggest poll topics before the live session. This not only boosts anticipation but also allows you to tailor the content to their interests.

Key Takeaways
- Choose a suitable platform for live sessions and promote them in advance.
- Foster a personal connection during live Q&A sessions by addressing participants by name.
- Integrate live polls to create an instant feedback loop and empower your audience.
- Use polls to guide the session's direction and involve your audience in decision-making.
- Build anticipation through pre-event announcements and engaging content preparation.

Chapter 8

Analyzing and Adjusting

Monitoring Instagram Insights

Hello, Analytics Explorer! In this chapter, we're delving into the crucial process of Monitoring Instagram Insights, a treasure trove of data that unveils the performance of your content, audience behavior, and the impact of your Instagram strategy. Let's unravel the art of data analysis to refine and adjust your approach for optimal results.

1. Navigate to Instagram Insights: The Data Compass
Access the Dashboard: Open the Instagram app and navigate to your business or creator profile. Tap on the Insights tab, your data compass guiding you through the intricacies of your Instagram universe.

Explore Overview Metrics: Begin with the Overview section to get a snapshot of your account's performance. Metrics like interactions, reach, and follower growth provide a quick glance at your Instagram landscape.

2. Dive into Content Insights: The Performance Canvas
Content Metrics: Explore the Content tab to analyze the performance of individual posts, stories, and IGTV. Identify top-performing content based on engagement, reach, and interactions.

Content Timing: Scrutinize the "When Your Followers Are Online" section to discover the optimal times for posting. Adjust your posting schedule to align with peak activity periods for maximum visibility.

3. Understand Audience Insights: The Connection Map
Follower Demographics: Head to the Audience tab to understand your follower demographics. Analyze age, gender, location, and the times when your audience is most active. Tailor your content to resonate with this profile.

Follower Growth: Track your follower growth over time. Identify periods of significant growth or decline and correlate them with specific content or campaigns. This insight informs your future strategy.

4. Explore Activity Insights: The Engagement Symphony
Interactions Overview: Examine the Interactions tab to understand how users are engaging with your content.

Metrics like profile visits, website clicks, and email clicks reveal the effectiveness of your call-to-action elements.

Discover Reach and Impressions: Uncover the reach and impressions of your content. Evaluate the effectiveness of hashtags, explore page interactions, and collaborations contributing to broader exposure.

5. Analyze Instagram Stories: The Snapshot Gallery
Story Metrics: Dedicate attention to your Instagram Stories. Analyze metrics like reach, taps forward, taps backward, and exits to understand the flow and impact of your stories. Identify trends and adjust your story content accordingly.

Engagement Stickers: Leverage insights into interactions with stickers (polls, questions, quizzes). Identify the types of stickers resonating most with your audience and incorporate them strategically.

6. Adjust Your Strategy: The Iterative Cycle
Identify Patterns and Trends: Look for patterns and trends in the data. Identify content themes, posting times, or engagement tactics that consistently yield positive results. Double down on what works.

Refine Content Approach: Based on audience demographics and content performance, refine your content approach. Tailor your messaging, visual style, and post frequency to align with your audience's preferences.

Adapt Posting Schedule: Utilize insights into when your audience is most active to adapt your posting schedule. Experiment with posting at different times and observe the impact on engagement.

Key Takeaways
- Use Instagram Insights to access a comprehensive overview of your account's performance.
- Analyze content performance, follower demographics, and audience engagement.
- Adjust your strategy based on identified patterns and trends.
- Refine your content approach and adapt your posting schedule for optimal results.

Analyzing Key Metrics for Growth

Greetings, Growth Alchemist! In this chapter, we embark on the enlightening journey of Analyzing Key Metrics for Growth. These metrics are the compass guiding you through the vast landscape of data, unveiling insights that hold the key to optimizing your strategies and fostering sustainable growth.

1. Follower Growth: The Audience Symphony
Evaluate Your Tribe: Monitor the growth of your follower count over time. Identify periods of significant growth and correlate them with specific campaigns, collaborations, or content themes. The trajectory of your follower count unveils the resonance of your content with your target audience.

Quality vs. Quantity: It's not just about the numbers. Assess the quality of your followers by considering engagement rates, interactions, and the alignment of their interests with your brand. A devoted, engaged audience is the catalyst for enduring growth.

2. Engagement Rates: The Interaction Pulse
Quantify Interactions: Dive into the metrics that quantify user interactions. Evaluate likes, comments, shares, and saves. High engagement rates signify content

resonance, while low rates may signal a need for content refinement.

Per-Post Analysis: Break down engagement rates on a per-post basis. Identify the types of content, captions, or visuals that consistently elicit higher engagement. Use these insights to craft content that resonates more effectively.

3. Reach and Impressions: The Visibility Canvas
Evaluate Reach: Examine the total number of unique accounts that have seen your content. Reach provides insight into the size of your potential audience. An increasing reach indicates expanded visibility.

Impressions Analysis: Delve into impressions to understand the total number of times your content has been viewed, including multiple views by the same user. High impressions with consistent engagement showcase content that captures attention.

4. Hashtag Performance: The Discoverability Elixir
Hashtag Reach and Engagement: Scrutinize the performance of your hashtags. Assess the reach and engagement metrics associated with specific hashtags. Identify which hashtags contribute most effectively to the discoverability of your content.

Optimize Hashtag Strategy: Experiment with different sets of hashtags and monitor their impact. Keep an eye on trending and niche-specific hashtags. A strategic hashtag approach can amplify your content's reach to broader audiences.

5. Website Clicks: The Conversion Trail
Track Click-Through Rates: If you have external links in your bio or posts, track the click-through rates. Analyze which call-to-actions (CTAs) resonate most with your audience. Optimize the placement and frequency of CTAs to encourage website clicks.

Conversion Analysis: Assess the effectiveness of your Instagram strategy in driving traffic to your website or landing pages. Track the performance of specific campaigns or promotional links to measure conversion rates.

6. Story Metrics: The Evolving Narrative
Story Engagement: Evaluate metrics related to your Instagram Stories. Analyze taps forward, taps backward, and exits. Identify patterns in user interactions to refine your storytelling approach and create more compelling stories.

Interactive Elements: Explore the engagement generated by interactive story elements such as polls, questions, and quizzes. Identify which elements resonate most with your audience and incorporate them strategically to enhance engagement.

Key Takeaways
- Monitor follower growth and assess the quality of your audience.
- Evaluate engagement rates on posts to gauge content resonance.
- Analyze reach and impressions to understand content visibility.
- Scrutinize hashtag performance for effective discoverability.
- Track website clicks to measure the impact on external traffic.
- Assess story metrics to refine your storytelling strategy.

Analyzing key metrics for growth is an ongoing practice of refinement and adaptation. In the next chapter, we'll explore the intricate world of Instagram Stories and how to craft narratives that captivate your audience. Get ready for a journey into the realm of visual storytelling!

Adjusting Your Strategy Based on Data

Greetings, Strategy Navigator! In this chapter, we're diving into the art of Adjusting Your Strategy Based on Data, a pivotal skill that transforms insights into actionable steps for sustainable growth. Let's navigate the data seas together and steer your Instagram ship toward strategic success.

1. Identify Patterns and Trends: The Data Constellations

Charting the Landscape: Dive into your Instagram Insights to identify patterns and trends within your data. Look for recurring themes in high-performing content, posting times, and audience engagement. These patterns are the constellations guiding your strategic navigation.

Analyze Peaks and Valleys: Examine periods of significant growth or decline. Correlate these with specific campaigns, content types, or external factors. Understanding the context behind peaks and valleys empowers you to replicate success and mitigate challenges.

2. Content Performance Analysis: The Impactful Composition

Top-Performing Content: Identify your top-performing content based on engagement metrics. Assess the visual elements, captions, and themes that resonate most with your audience. These insights lay the foundation for refining your content strategy.

Content Themes and Variations: Explore the performance of content with specific themes or variations. Identify the sweet spots, topics or styles that consistently capture attention. Leverage these insights to craft a content mix that maintains diversity while catering to audience preferences.

3. Audience Demographics Refinement: The Connection Optimization
Demographic Insights: Scrutinize the demographics of your audience. Are there specific age groups, locations, or genders that engage more with your content? Refine your target audience based on these insights, ensuring your content aligns with the interests of your core demographic.

Adaptation for Growth: As your audience evolves, adapt your content approach to cater to changing demographics. This iterative adaptation ensures your strategy remains aligned with the evolving preferences of your audience.

4. Hashtag Strategy Optimization: The Visibility Fine-Tuning

Top-Performing Hashtags: Identify the hashtags that consistently contribute to content visibility and engagement. Fine-tune your hashtag strategy by emphasizing those that align with your brand and have a proven track record of effectiveness.

Experimentation and Rotation: Continue experimenting with new hashtags to discover untapped audiences. Rotate and diversify your hashtag usage to prevent stagnation and maintain a fresh approach to content discoverability.

5. Adapt to Algorithm Changes: The Algorithm Dance

Stay Informed: Keep abreast of changes in the Instagram algorithm. Platforms frequently update algorithms, impacting content visibility and engagement. Staying informed allows you to adjust your strategy in response to algorithmic shifts.

Algorithm-Centric Strategies: Tailor your content strategy to align with algorithm preferences. Whether it's prioritizing certain content formats, engagement features, or post frequencies, aligning with the algorithm enhances your content's chances of visibility.

6. Iterative Refinement: The Strategy Evolution

Continuous Improvement Mindset: Embrace a mindset of continuous improvement. Your Instagram strategy is a living entity that evolves with your brand, audience, and platform dynamics. Regularly revisit and refine your strategy based on ongoing data insights.

Test and Learn: Implement a test-and-learn approach. Experiment with variations in content, posting schedules, and engagement tactics. Use data to assess the impact of these experiments and integrate successful elements into your long-term strategy.

Key Takeaways
- Identify patterns and trends in your Instagram data.
- Analyze top-performing content for impactful insights.
- Refine your target audience based on demographic data.
- Optimize your hashtag strategy for enhanced visibility.
- Adapt your strategy to changes in the Instagram algorithm.
- Embrace a continuous improvement mindset for strategic evolution.

Chapter 9

Troubleshooting Common Challenges

Dealing with Algorithm Changes

Hello, Algorithm Navigator! In this chapter, we're setting sail into the digital currents and addressing one of the common challenges every Instagram strategist faces, Dealing with Algorithm Changes. As the algorithmic tides ebb and flow, let's equip ourselves with strategies to navigate these changes and ensure your content continues to ride the waves of visibility.

1. Stay Informed: The Algorithmic Compass
Continuous Awareness: Algorithms are the invisible currents shaping your Instagram journey. Stay informed about algorithm updates, changes, and announcements from Instagram. Regularly check official sources and reputable industry publications to stay ahead of the curve.

Algorithm Release Notes: Explore release notes provided by Instagram when algorithm changes are introduced. These notes often contain valuable insights into the platform's evolving priorities, helping you align your content strategy accordingly.

2. Adaptability Mindset: The Strategy Evolution
Embrace Adaptability: The only constant in the digital landscape is change. Adopt an adaptability mindset within your content strategy. Recognize that algorithm changes are opportunities to evolve and refine your approach, rather than obstacles to overcome.

Iterative Refinement: View your strategy as an evolving entity. Regularly iterate, refine, and test different content approaches to align with algorithmic shifts. The ability to adapt swiftly ensures your content remains relevant and visible.

3. Diversify Content Formats: The Multimedia Palette
Explore Different Formats: Algorithms often favor specific content formats. Diversify your content palette by experimenting with a variety of formats, including photos, videos, carousels, and Stories. This not only caters to diverse audience preferences but also aligns with potential algorithmic priorities.

Storytelling Across Formats: Craft narratives that seamlessly transition across different formats. For example, leverage Instagram Stories to complement your main feed posts. This cohesive storytelling approach enhances engagement and aligns with potential algorithmic preferences.

4. Engage with New Features: The Feature Showcase
Early Adoption: Algorithms tend to favor new features and tools introduced by the platform. Be an early adopter of new Instagram features, whether it's IGTV, Reels, or interactive elements within Stories. Engaging with these features signals to the algorithm that you are embracing platform advancements.

Strategic Feature Integration: Strategically integrate new features into your content plan. Experiment with different functionalities and observe how your audience responds. Incorporate successful elements into your long-term strategy to align with potential algorithmic preferences.

5. Focus on Meaningful Engagement: The Connection Thread
Prioritize Authentic Interactions: Algorithms increasingly prioritize authentic and meaningful engagement over superficial metrics. Encourage genuine interactions, such as comments and shares, by creating content that sparks conversations. Meaningful engagement signals to the algorithm that your content is valuable to the community.

Community-Centric Approach: Foster a community-centric approach within your content strategy. Respond promptly to comments, ask questions, and create content that invites your audience to share their thoughts. A thriving community positively impacts algorithmic visibility.

6. Monitor Analytics Closely: The Data Lighthouse

Track Performance Metrics: Keep a vigilant eye on your Instagram Insights. Monitor performance metrics such as reach, impressions, and engagement. Track how these metrics evolve alongside algorithm changes to discern patterns and make informed adjustments.

Adapt Based on Analytics: Use insights derived from analytics to guide your content strategy adjustments. If certain types of content or posting schedules align with increased visibility, integrate these findings into your ongoing strategy. Data-driven adaptation is key.

Key Takeaways

- Stay informed about algorithm updates through official sources.
- Embrace adaptability within your content strategy to navigate changes.
- Diversify your content formats to align with potential algorithmic preferences.

- Engage with new features and tools introduced by the platform.
- Prioritize meaningful engagement to signal value to the algorithm.
- Monitor Instagram Insights closely to track performance metrics.

Overcoming Plateaus in Growth

Greetings, Growth Voyager! In this chapter, we embark on the journey of Overcoming Plateaus in Growth, a challenge faced by every intrepid Instagram explorer. Whether you're navigating a growth plateau or anticipating one, let's equip you with strategies to ascend to new heights and scale the summit of sustained growth.

1. Evaluate Content Performance: The Content Expedition

Content Analysis: Dive deep into the performance of your content. Identify top-performing posts and discern patterns in engagement. Assess the content themes, formats, and storytelling techniques that resonate most with your audience.

Refresh and Innovate: While maintaining consistency is crucial, injecting freshness into your content is equally vital. Experiment with new content formats, themes, and creative approaches. Innovate within the framework of what your audience finds compelling.

2. Reassess Target Audience: The Connection Compass

Demographic Refinement: Plateaus may indicate a misalignment with your target audience. Reassess and refine your understanding of your audience demographics. Ensure that your content speaks directly to the interests and preferences of your intended community.

Audience Surveys and Feedback: Directly engage with your audience through surveys, polls, and feedback requests. Gather insights into their evolving preferences, interests, and expectations. Incorporate this feedback into your content strategy for a more targeted approach.

3. Collaborate and Cross-Promote: The Community Network

Strategic Collaborations: Leverage the power of collaborations with other content creators, influencers, or brands. Collaborative efforts can introduce your content to new audiences and breathe fresh energy into your growth strategy.

Cross-Promotion Tactics: Explore cross-promotion opportunities on various social media platforms or within niche communities. Cross-promoting with aligned entities can expand your reach and attract diverse audiences interested in your content.

4. Optimize Hashtag Strategy: The Visibility Beacon

Hashtag Overhaul: Revamp your hashtag strategy by exploring new, trending, and niche-specific hashtags. Optimize the mix of popular and less competitive hashtags to enhance the discoverability of your content.

Hashtags are the beacons that guide users to your content.

Community Engagement Through Hashtags: Create or participate in community-driven hashtags that align with your content theme. Encourage your audience to use these hashtags, fostering a sense of community and increasing the visibility of your content within specific circles.

5. *Diversify Content Platforms: The Multichannel Odyssey*
Explore Multichannel Presence: Consider expanding your presence beyond Instagram. Explore other platforms that align with your content style and audience demographics. Platforms like YouTube, TikTok, or Pinterest may provide additional avenues for growth.

Cross-Platform Synergy: Develop a strategy that integrates and cross-promotes content across multiple platforms. A synergistic approach ensures that your content reaches diverse audiences while maintaining a cohesive brand presence.

6. *Engage with Trends and Challenges: The Trendsetter's Leap*
Trend Integration: Stay attuned to current trends and challenges within your niche. Integrating trending topics

into your content not only keeps it relevant but can also attract new audiences following popular trends.

Challenge Participation: Engage in viral challenges or trends relevant to your content theme. Participation not only positions you within ongoing conversations but also exposes your profile to users actively exploring trending content.

Key Takeaways
- Evaluate and innovate your content to keep it fresh and engaging.
- Reassess and refine your understanding of your target audience.
- Leverage collaborations and cross-promotions for expanded reach.
- Optimize your hashtag strategy to enhance content discoverability.
- Explore multichannel presence for additional growth opportunities.
- Engage with current trends and challenges to stay relevant.

Handling Negative Comments and Feedback

Greetings, Resilience Navigator! In this chapter, we're delving into the delicate yet empowering topic of Handling Negative Comments and Feedback. Just like a ship facing rough seas, your ability to navigate through criticism will define the strength of your brand. Let's equip you with strategies to weather the storms and emerge stronger.

1. Embrace a Calm Response: The Diplomat's Approach

Pause and Reflect: When faced with negativity, take a moment to pause before responding. Allow yourself time to process the feedback without an immediate emotional reaction. This thoughtful pause forms the foundation for a composed response.

Respond with Empathy: Craft your response with empathy. Acknowledge the concerns raised and express understanding. Responding with empathy establishes a connection and demonstrates that you value your audience's perspective.

2. Address Legitimate Concerns: The Solution Architect

Separate Constructive Criticism: Distinguish between constructive criticism and unwarranted negativity. Address valid concerns by outlining steps you're taking to resolve the issue. Demonstrating a commitment to improvement showcases your dedication to delivering value.

Seek Clarification: If the feedback is unclear, seek clarification. A polite request for more information not only shows your willingness to engage but also allows you to better understand the nature of the concern.

3. Take Conversations Privately: The Personal Connection

Move to Direct Messages: Encourage further discussion through private channels. This demonstrates your commitment to resolving the issue and prevents a public escalation. Direct messages provide a more personal space for addressing concerns.

Maintain Professionalism: Even in private conversations, uphold a professional tone. Confidentiality doesn't mean compromising your brand's image. Ensure that your responses are respectful and solution-oriented.

4. Establish Community Guidelines: The Rulebook

Transparent Guidelines: Clearly communicate community guidelines on your platform. This sets expectations for acceptable behavior and content. Having transparent guidelines allows you to refer users back to established rules when necessary.

Moderate Effectively: Actively moderate your platform to ensure adherence to guidelines. Address inappropriate comments promptly to maintain a positive community atmosphere. A well-moderated space fosters respectful interactions.

5. Use Humor Wisely: The Tactful Jester

Light-Hearted Responses: In some cases, humor can defuse tension. If appropriate, respond with light-heartedness to negative comments. This approach can disarm negativity and showcase your ability to handle criticism gracefully.

Avoid Sarcasm: Exercise caution with humor to ensure it doesn't come across as dismissive or sarcastic.

Maintain a balance between levity and sincerity to prevent further escalation.

6. Learn and Improve: The Growth Mindset

Extract Learning Points: Negative feedback often harbors valuable insights. Extract learning points from criticism to identify areas for improvement. Embrace a growth mindset that views challenges as opportunities for development.

Adapt Strategies: Use the feedback to adapt and refine your strategies. Continuous improvement based on user feedback not only strengthens your brand but also fosters a sense of community involvement.

Key Takeaways
- Respond to negativity with a composed and empathetic approach.
- Address legitimate concerns by outlining steps for improvement.
- Encourage private conversations for more personalized resolution.
- Establish and communicate transparent community guidelines.
- Use humor wisely to defuse tension when appropriate.

- Extract learning points and adapt strategies for continuous improvement.

Handling negative comments and feedback is an art of resilience, turning challenges into opportunities for growth. In the next chapter, let's explore the realm of Instagram Analytics and how data-driven insights can elevate your content strategy. Get ready for a data-driven journey!

Conclusion

Congratulations, Instagram Explorer, on completing this captivating journey through "How to Get Your First 1,000 Instagram Followers"! As you close the final chapter of this guide, you've not only gained insights into growing your Instagram presence but have also uncovered the secrets to navigating the intricate terrain of the ever-evolving digital landscape.

Throughout this odyssey, we've explored the art of creating a compelling Instagram profile, crafting visually stunning content, developing a robust content strategy, mastering the hashtag game, leveraging influencer collaborations, riding the waves of viral trends, engaging with your audience, and analyzing key metrics for strategic growth.

In the world of Instagram, where trends shift like sand dunes and algorithms evolve like seasons, your newfound knowledge is your compass. You've learned to adjust your strategy based on data, troubleshoot common challenges, and handle the occasional storm of negative feedback with grace.

Remember, your Instagram journey is not a sprint but a marathon. Plateaus will test your resilience, algorithm changes will challenge your adaptability, and negative comments will be storms to navigate. Yet, armed with the strategies and insights from this guide, you're well-equipped to turn challenges into opportunities, transforming setbacks into stepping stones towards your Instagram goals.

As you step back into the vibrant realm of Instagram, bring with you the spirit of innovation, the wisdom of data-driven decisions, and the resilience to weather any storm. Your Instagram odyssey is uniquely yours, and the story you tell through your profile is a narrative waiting to unfold.

May your content continue to inspire, your community flourish, and your Instagram journey be filled with growth, authenticity, and moments of creative brilliance. Cheers to your ongoing success on this captivating platform!

Safe travels, Instagram Explorer. Your adventure continues, and the best chapters are yet to be written.

Happy Instagramming!.

Printed in Great Britain
by Amazon